Preparatory

Mid-Elementary

A DOZEN A DAY
CHRISTMAS

Orchestrated Accompaniments by Eric Baumgartner

The price of this publication includes access to audio tracks online for download or streaming, using the unique code below.

To access audio, visit:
www.halleonard.com/mylibrary

Enter Code
3502-9192-7202-4430

ISBN 978-1-4950-2689-8

EXCLUSIVELY DISTRIBUTED BY

Visit Hal Leonard Online at
www.halleonard.com

Contact us:
Hal Leonard
7777 West Bluemound Road
Milwaukee, WI 53213
Email: info@halleonard.com

In Europe, contact:
Hal Leonard Europe Limited
42 Wigmore Street
Marylebone, London, W1U 2RN
Email: info@halleonardeurope.com

In Australia, contact:
Hal Leonard Australia Pty. Ltd.
4 Lentara Court
Cheltenham, Victoria, 3192 Australia
Email: info@halleonard.com.au

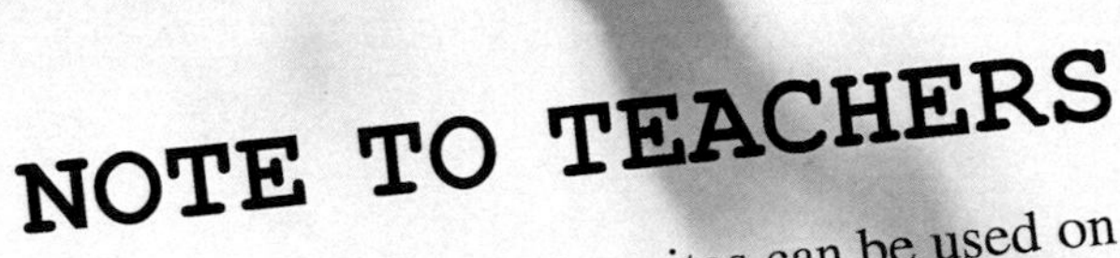

NOTE TO TEACHERS

This collection of Christmas favorites can be used on its own or as supplementary material to the iconic *A Dozen A Day* technique series by Edna Mae Burnam. The pieces have been arranged to progress gradually, applying concepts and patterns from Burnam's technical exercises whenever possible. Optional accompaniments are also provided for teachers or older students.

These arrangements are excellent supplements for any method and may also be used for sight-reading practice for more advanced students.

SUGGESTED ORDER OF STUDY

The First Noël

17th Century English Carol
Music from W. Sandys' *Christmas Carols*
Arranged by Carolyn Miller

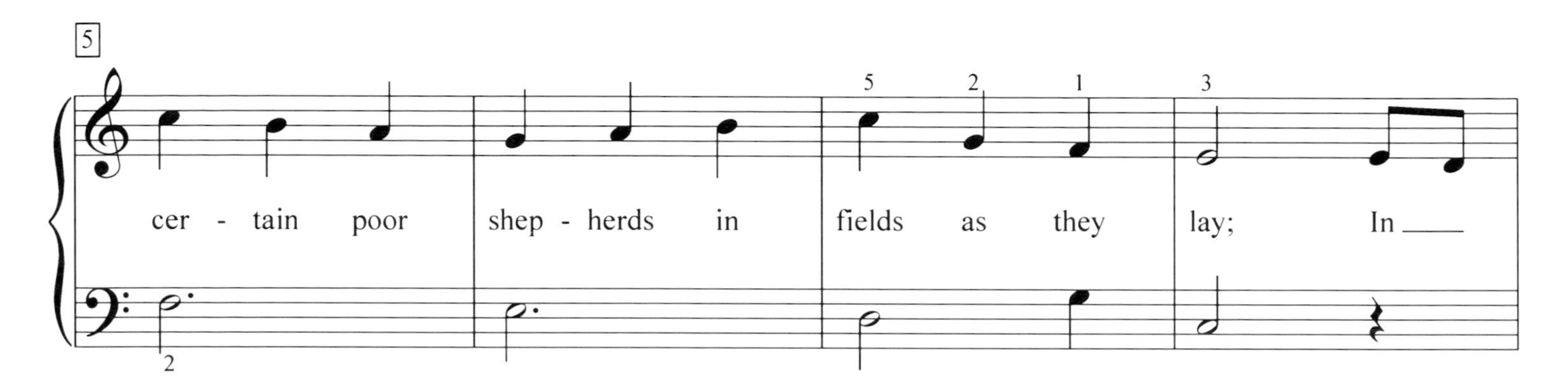

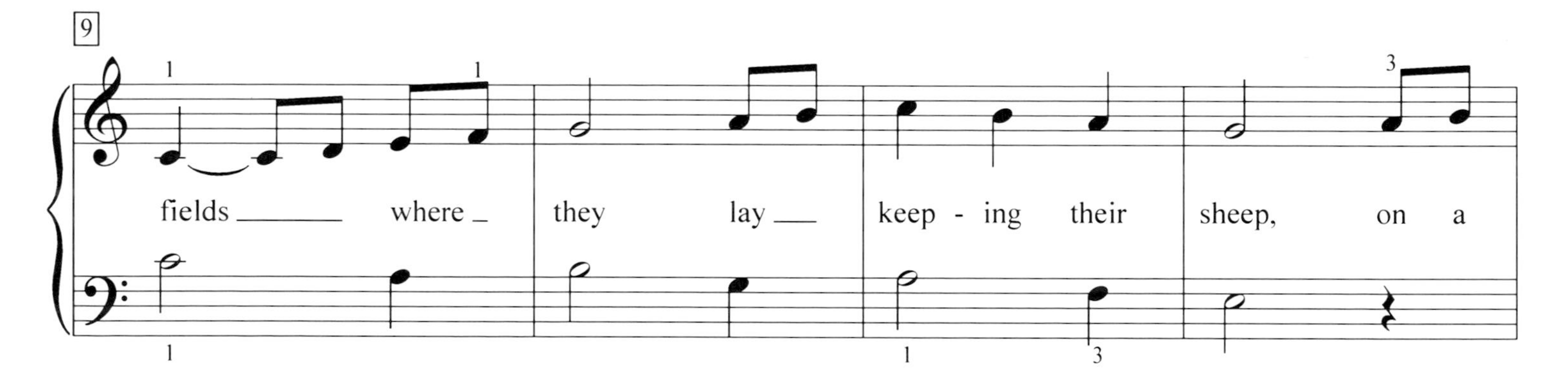

Accompaniment (Student plays one octave higher than written.)

13
cold win - ter's night that was so deep. No -

17
ël, No - ël, No - ël, No - ël,

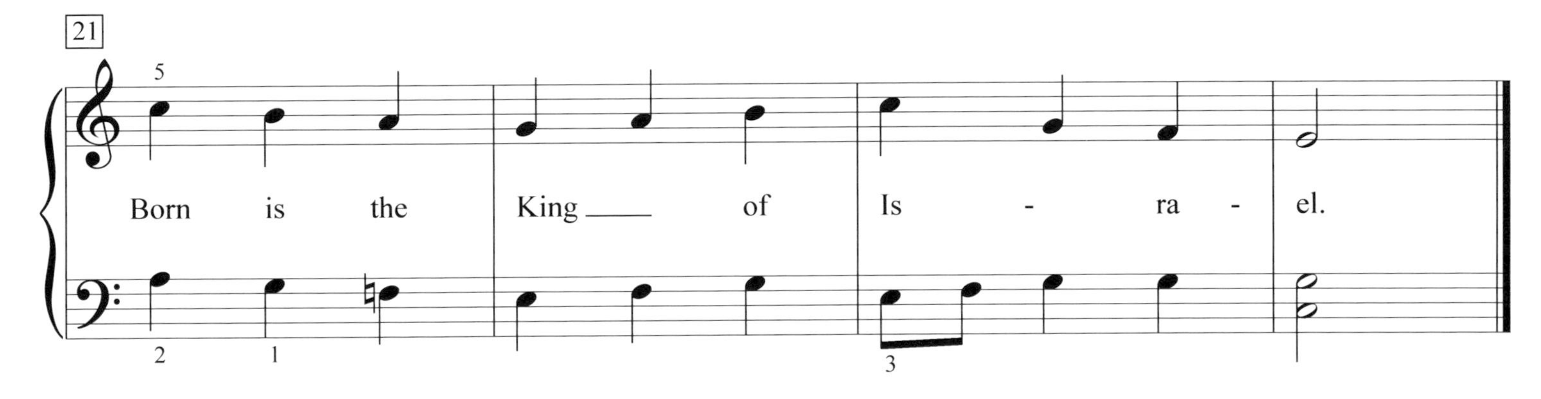
21
Born is the King of Is - ra - el.

13
17
21

This page is intentionally left blank
to avoid unnecessary page turns.

Jingle, Jingle, Jingle

Music and Lyrics by
Johnny Marks
Arranged by Carolyn Miller

Accompaniment (Student plays one octave higher than written.)

13
They are not just plain deer, they're the fast - est deer I

16
know. You must be - lieve that on Christ - mas Eve

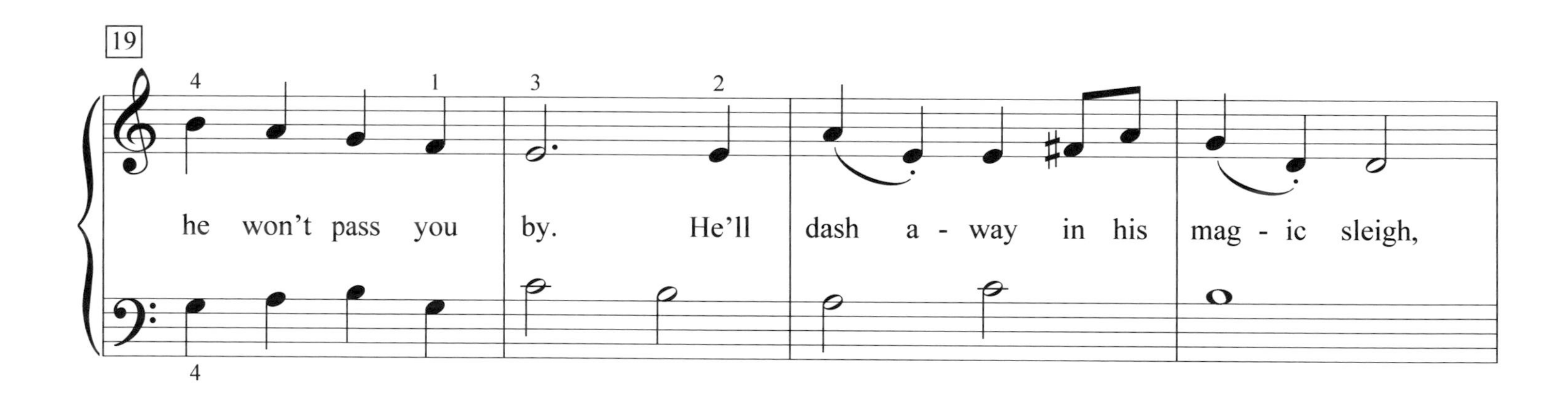
19
he won't pass you by. He'll dash a - way in his mag - ic sleigh,

13
16
19

23
1
fly - ing through the sky.
Jin - gle, jin - gle, jin - gle, you will

27
1
hear his sleigh - bells ring.
Jol - ly old Kris Krin - gle is the

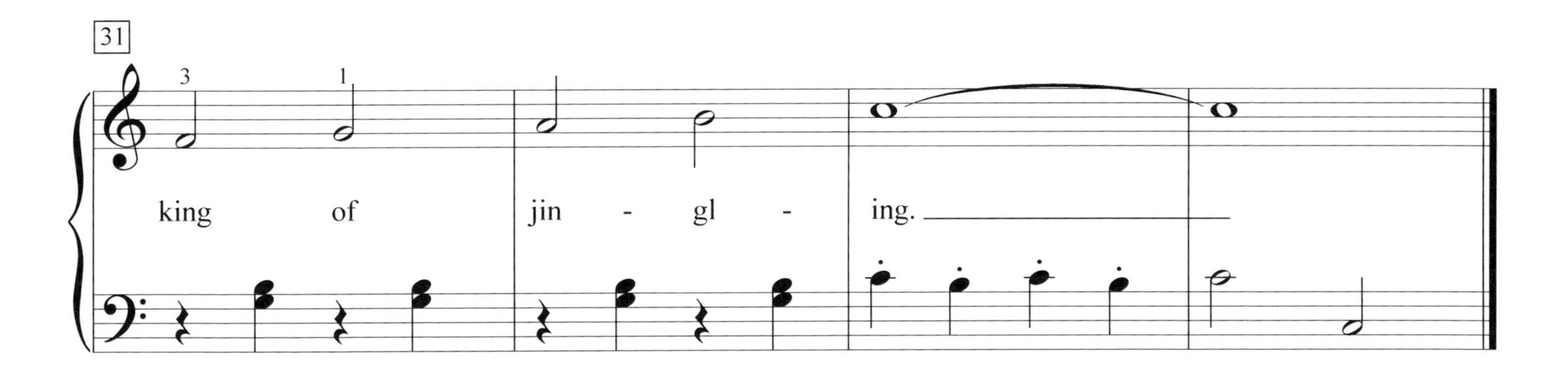
31
3
1
king of jin - gl - ing.

23
27
31

Joy to the World

Words by Isaac Watts
Music by George Frideric Handel
Adapted by Lowell Mason
Arranged by Carolyn Miller

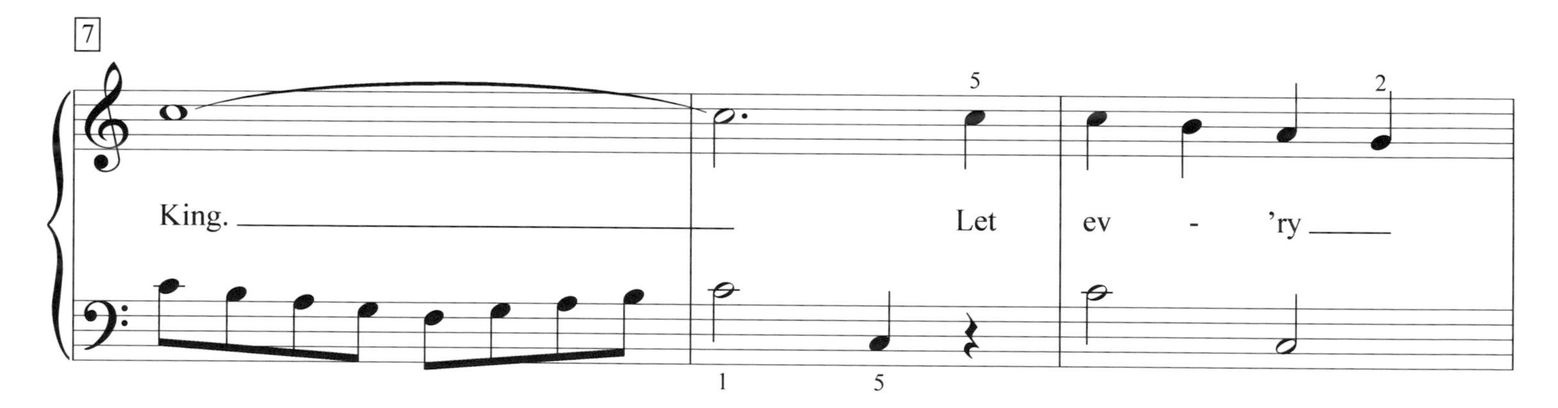

Accompaniment (Student plays one octave higher than written.)

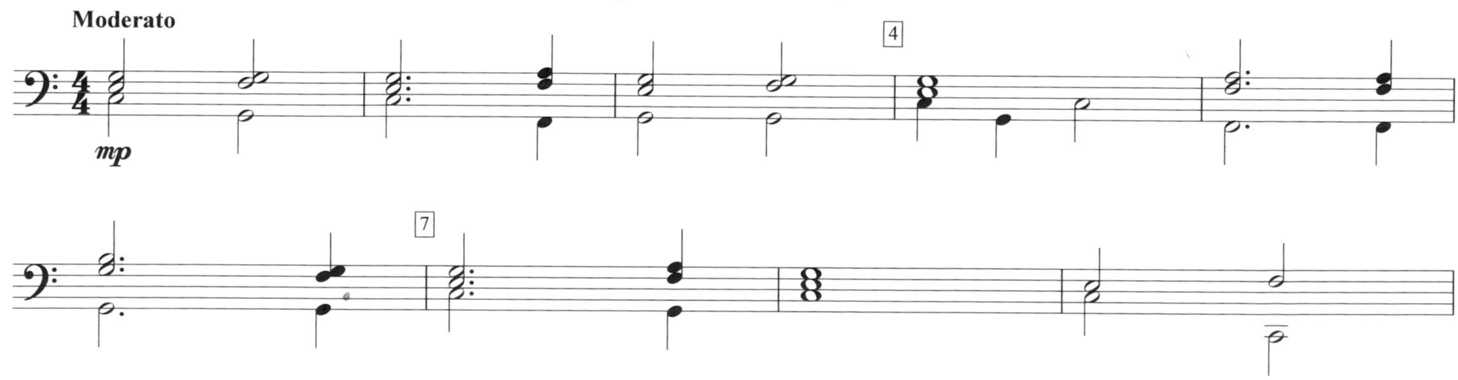

10
heart pre - pare Him room, and

13
heav'n and na - ture sing, and heav'n and na - ture sing, and

17
heav'n and heav'n and na - ture sing.

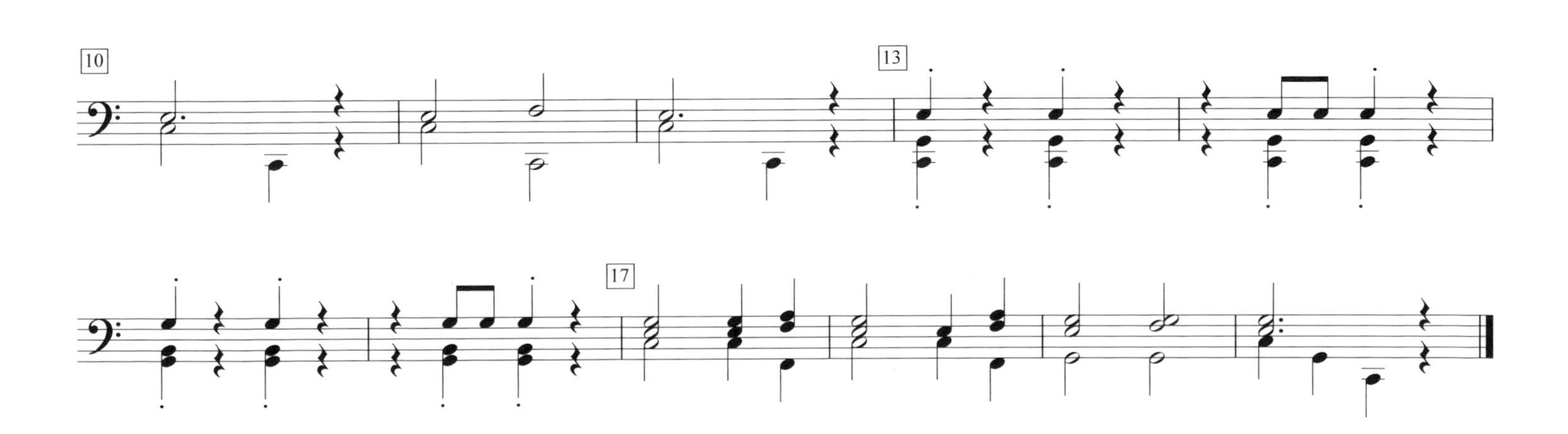
10
13
17

Here Comes Santa Claus
(Right Down Santa Claus Lane)

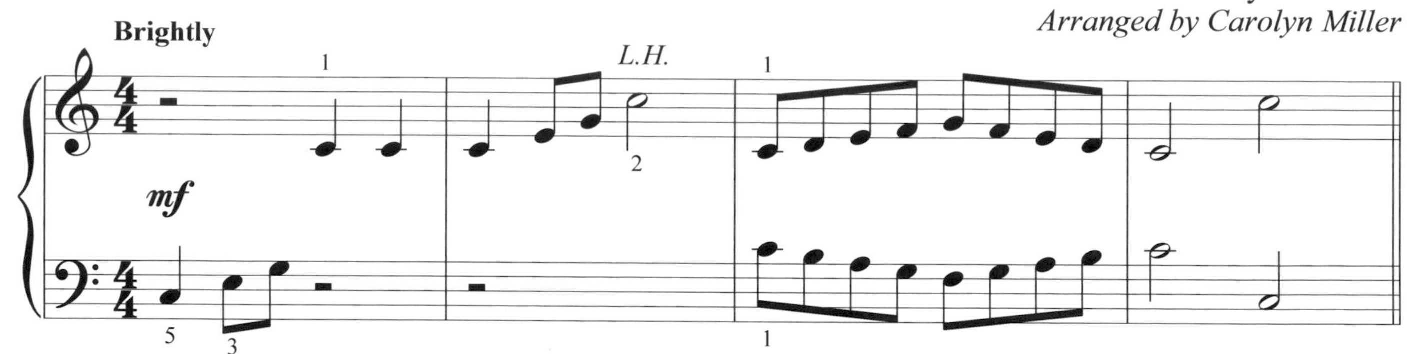

Accompaniment (Student plays one octave higher than written.)

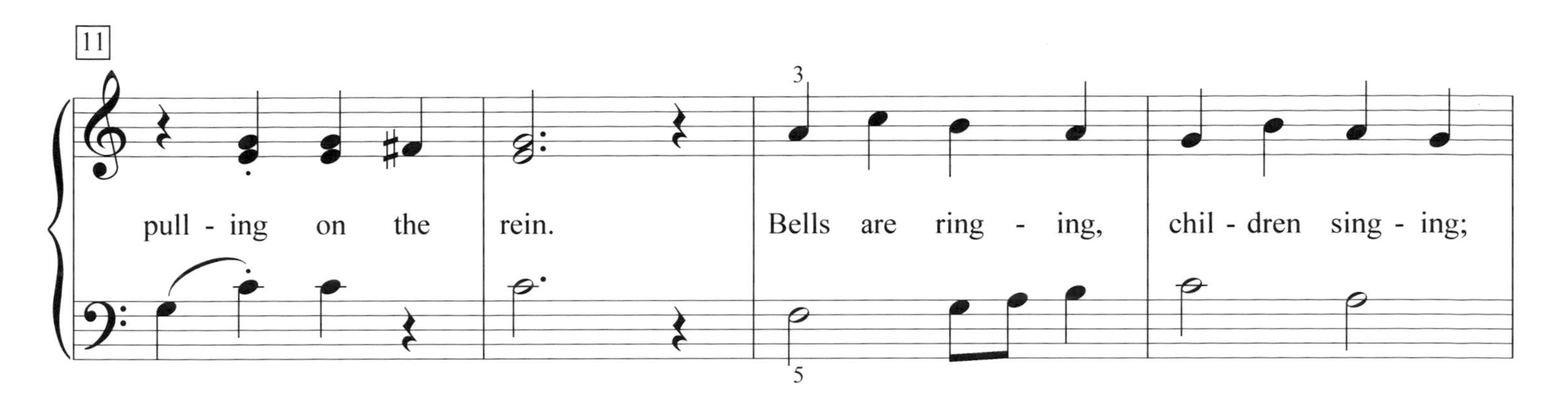
11
3
pull - ing on the rein. Bells are ring - ing, chil - dren sing - ing;
5

15
1 1 3 3
all is mer - ry and bright. Hang your stock - ings and
1 1 5

18
1 5
say your prayers 'cause San - ta Claus comes to - night.

11
15
18

The Little Drummer Boy

Words and Music by Harry Simeone,
Henry Onorati and Katherine Davis
Arranged by Carolyn Miller

Accompaniment (Student plays one octave higher than written.)

15
4 3 2
3
to set be - fore the King, pa rum pum pum pum, rum pum pum pum,

19
rum pum pum pum, so to hon - or Him, pa

23
rum pum pum pum, when we come.

15
19
23

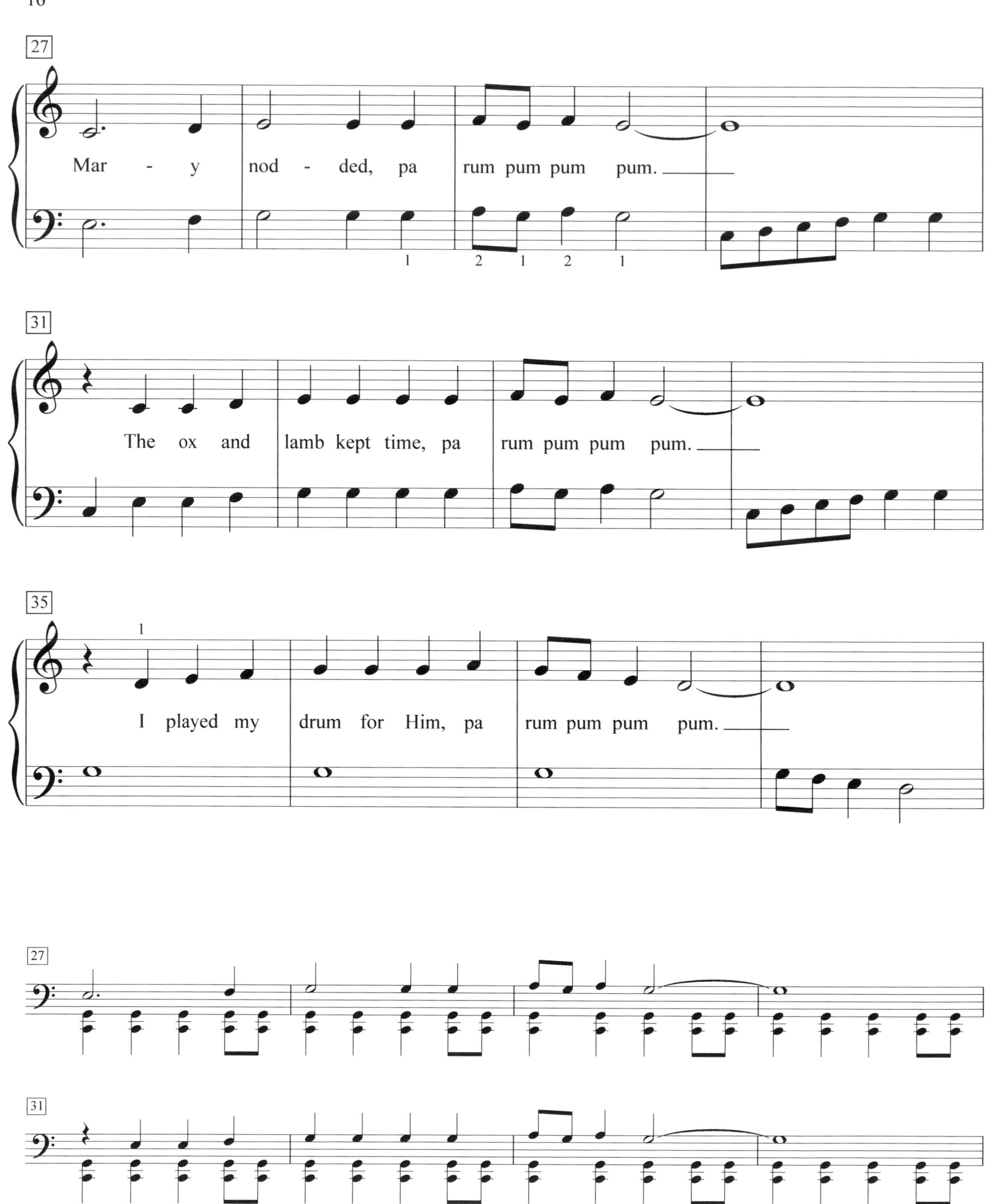
27
Mar - y nod - ded, pa rum pum pum pum.
1 2 1 2 1
31
The ox and lamb kept time, pa rum pum pum pum.
35
1
I played my drum for Him, pa rum pum pum pum.
27
31
35

39
4 3 2
3
I played my best for Him, pa rum pum pum pum, rum pum pum pum,
43
rum pum pum pum.
Then He
48
smiled at me, pa rum pum pum pum,
me and my drum.
39
43
48

Do You Hear What I Hear

Words and Music by Noel Regney
and Gloria Shayne
Arranged by Carolyn Miller

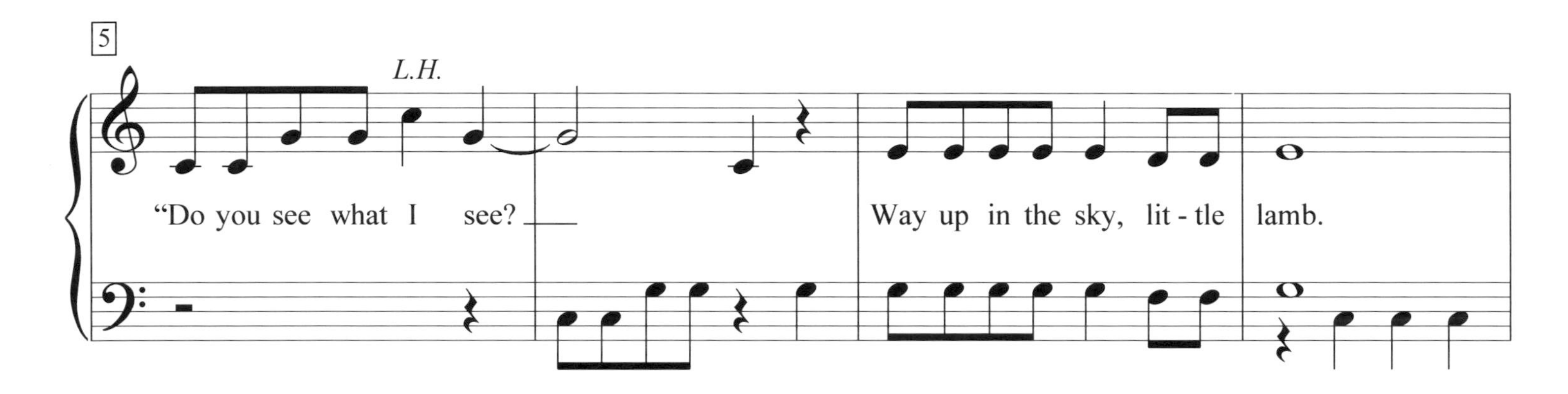

Accompaniment (Student plays one octave higher than written.)

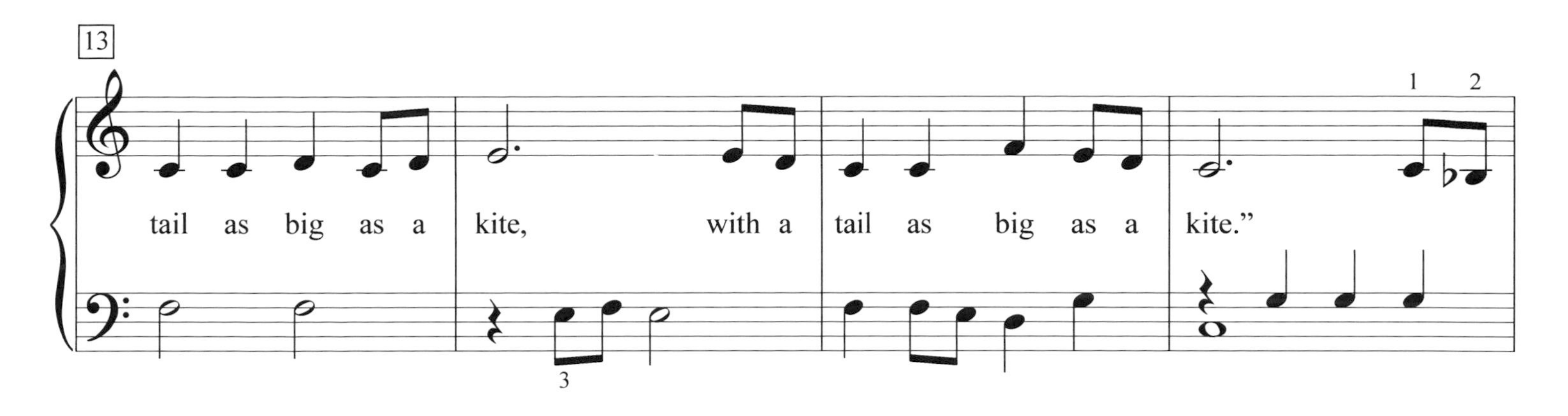
13
1 2
tail as big as a kite, with a tail as big as a kite."
3

17
1
L.H.
Said the lit-tle lamb to the shep-herd boy, "Do you hear what I hear?
mf

21
Ring-ing through the sky, shep-herd boy.

13
17
21
mp

24
L.H.
4
Do you hear what I hear? A song, a song
f
2

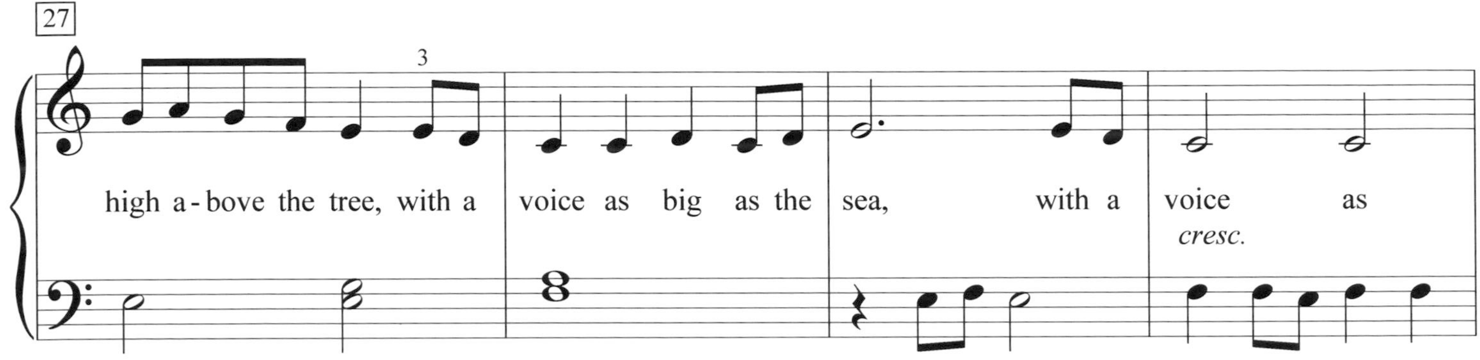
27
3
high a-bove the tree, with a voice as big as the sea, with a voice as
cresc.

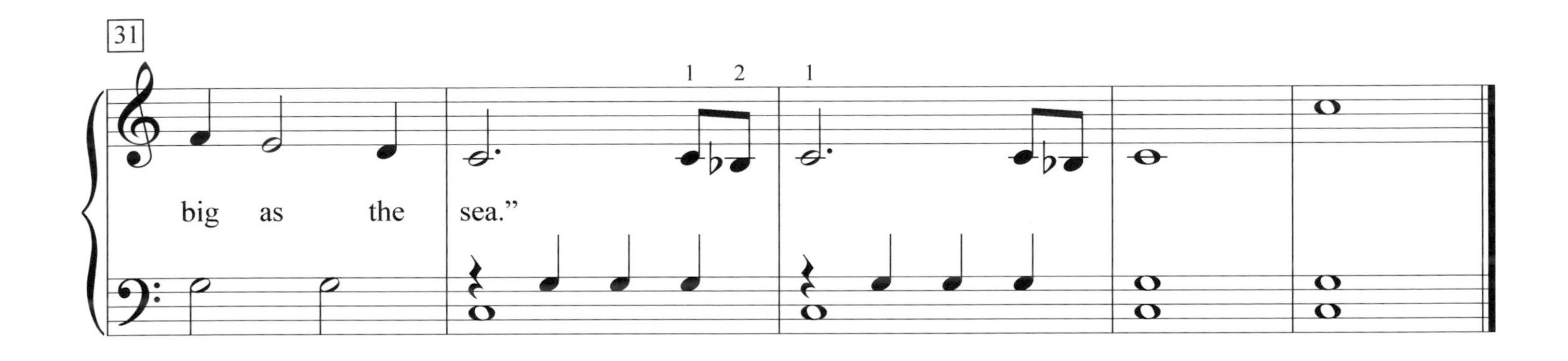
31
1 2 1
big as the sea."

24
mf
27
cresc.
31

Rockin' Around the Christmas Tree

Music and Lyrics by
Johnny Marks
Arranged by Carolyn Miller

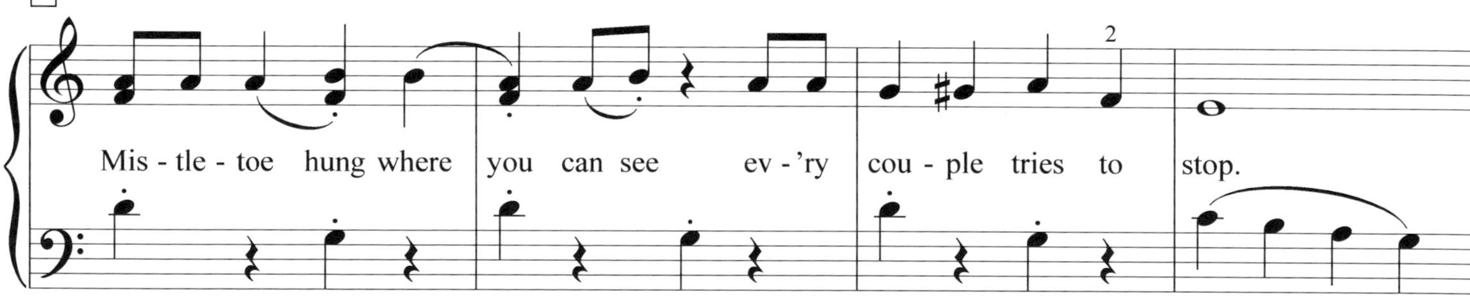

Accompaniment (Student plays one octave higher than written.)

13
Rock - in' a - round the Christ - mas tree, let the Christ - mas spir - it
16
ring. Lat - er we'll have some pump - kin pie and we'll
19
do some car - ol - ing. You will get a sen - ti - men - tal
23
feel - ing when you hear voic - es sing - ing, "Let's be jol - ly,
13
16
19
23

27
deck the halls with boughs of hol - ly."
Rock - in' a - round the
30
Christ - mas tree, have a hap - py hol - i - day.
33
Ev - 'ry - one danc - ing mer - ri - ly in the new old - fash - ioned
36
way.
27
30
33
36

White Christmas

from the Motion Picture Irving Berlin's HOLIDAY INN

Words and Music by
Irving Berlin
Arranged by Carolyn Miller

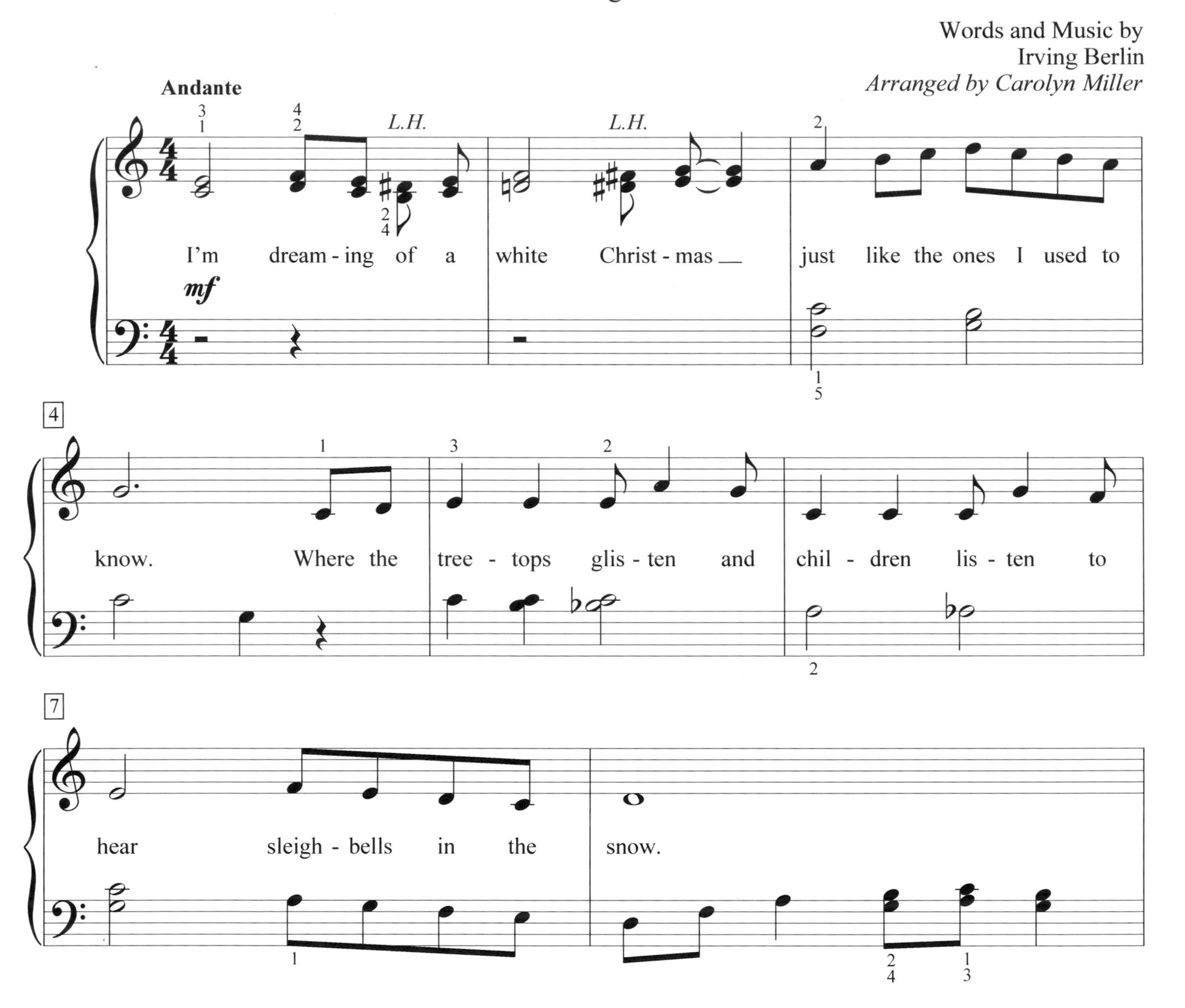

Accompaniment (Student plays one octave higher than written.)

9
L.H.
L.H.
I'm dream-ing of a white Christ-mas
with ev-'ry Christ-mas card I
12
write. May your days be mer-ry and bright, and may
rit.

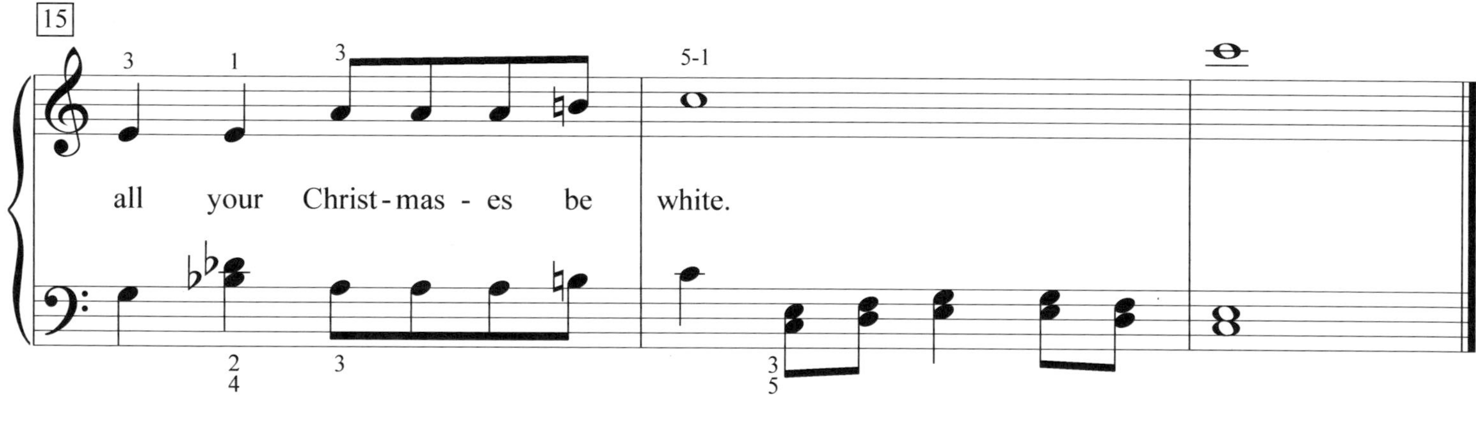
15
all your Christ-mas-es be white.

9
12
rit.
15

Christmas Is

Lyrics by Spence Maxwell
Music by Percy Faith
Arranged by Carolyn Miller

Accompaniment (Student plays one octave higher than written.)

9
3
Christ - mas is mem - 'ries, the kind you _ al - ways keep. Deck the halls and _ give a
3

12
3
cheer _____ for all the things that Christ - mas is each year. Christ - mas, Mer - ry

16
3
1
Christ - mas, when all your wish - es come true. Christ - mas is car - ols to
3

9
12
16
3

20
warm you _ in the snow;
Christ - mas is bed - time, where
no one _ wants to go.

23
All the world is ___ tin - sel
bright, ___ so glad to
know that Christ - mas is to -
night.

27
L.H.
Christ - mas, Mer - ry
Christ - mas, when
all your wish - es come
true.

20
23
27

The Christmas Song

(Chestnuts Roasting on an Open Fire)

Music and Lyric by Mel Tormé
and Robert Wells
Arranged by Carolyn Miller

13
help to make the sea - son
bright.
Ti - ny tots with their
16
eyes all a - glow will
find it hard to sleep to -
night. They know that
19
San - ta's on his
way; he's load - ed
lots of toys and good - ies on his
22
sleigh. And ev - 'ry
moth - er's child is gon - na
spy to see if

25
rein - deer real - ly know how to fly. And so I'm of - fer - ing this
28
sim - ple phrase to kids from one to nine - ty - two. Al -
31
though it's been said man - y times, man - y ways, "Mer - ry Christ - mas, Mer - ry
rit.
34
Christ - mas, Mer - ry Christ - mas to you."
25
28
31
rit.
34

Celebrate Christmas with Willis Music

Elementary

STEP BY STEP CHRISTMAS SONGBOOK – BOOK 1

Glenda Austin
Early Elementary

10 solos: Bells Are Ringing • Good King Wenceslas • I Saw Three Ships • Jingle Bells • Jolly Old St. Nicholas • O Come, Little Children • O Come, O Come, Emmanuel • One Shining Star • Snowing, Snowing! • While Shepherds Watched Their Flocks.

00278591 Book/Online Audio..........$9.99

TEACHING LITTLE FINGERS TO PLAY CHRISTMAS CAROLS

arr. Carolyn Miller
Early Elementary

12 solos: Angels We Have Heard on High • Deck the Hall • The First Noel • Hark! The Herald Angels Sing • Jingle Bells • Jolly Old Saint Nicholas • Joy to the World! • O Come, All Ye Faithful • O Come Little Children • Silent Night • Up on the Housetop • We Three Kings of Orient Are.

00406391..........$8.99

A YOUNG PIANIST'S FIRST CHRISTMAS

arr. William Gillock
Early Elementary

8 solos: Away in a Manger • Good King Wenceslas • Hark! The Herald Angels Sing • Jingle Bells • Jolly Old Saint Nicholas • Joy to the World • O Come, All Ye Faithful • Silent Night.

00416048..........$6.99

CHRISTMAS CAROLS FOR KIDS

arr. Carolyn C. Setliff
Elementary to Mid-Elementary

10 solos: The First Noel • Hark! the Herald Angels Sing • I Saw Three Ships • Jingle Bells • Joseph Dearest, Joseph Mine • Joy to the World • O Come, All Ye Faithful (Adeste Fideles) • Pat-A-Pan (Willie, Take Your Little Drum) • Silent Night • Up on the Housetop.

00237250..........$7.99

FIRST CHRISTMAS HITS

arr. Carolyn Miller
Mid to Later Elementary

8 solos: All I Want for Christmas Is My Two Front Teeth • The Chipmunk Song • Feliz Navidad • Grandma Got Run over by a Reindeer • A Holly Jolly Christmas • Mister Santa • Somewhere in My Memory • Where Are You Christmas?

00128892..........$9.99

Prices, contents, and availability subject to change without notice.

MERRY CHRISTMAS!

arr. Carolyn Miller
Mid to Later Elementary

8 solos: Away in a Manger • Deck the Hall • The First Noel • It Came upon the Midnight Clear • Jingle Bells • Jolly Old St. Nicholas • Joy to the World • Silent Night.

00416914..........$7.99

CHRISTMAS TOGETHER

arr. William Gillock
Later Elementary to Early Intermediate Duets

20 duets: Angels We Have Heard on High • Away in a Manger • Jingle Bells • Lullay, Thou Little Tiny Child • O Christmas Tree • O Little Town of Bethlehem • Silent Night • Ukrainian Bell Carol • We Wish You a Merry Christmas • What Child Is This? • and more!

00237199..........$9.99

CHRISTMAS CREATIONS

arr. Randall Hartsell
Later Elementary

11 carols: Away in a Manger • Carol of the Bells • Deck the Hall • God Rest Ye Merry, Gentlemen • Jingle Bells • Joy to the World • O Come, Little Children • Silent Night • We Three Kings of Orient Are • and more.

00416823..........$8.99

THE JOHN THOMPSON BOOK OF CHRISTMAS CAROLS (2ND ED.)

arr. John Thompson
Later Elementary

Features lyrics, as well as the original illustrations by George Williams. 14 songs: Away in a Manger • Deck the Hall • The First Noel • Good King Wenceslas • Joy to the World • Silent Night • and more!

00414699..........$9.99

For more Christmas and other seasonal music, please visit www.willispianomusic.com

Exclusively Distributed By

Intermediate – Advanced

CHRISTMAS PIANO SOLOS

FOURTH GRADE

arr. Eric Baumgartner
Early to Mid-Intermediate

10 holiday favorites: Blue Christmas • The Christmas Song (Chestnuts Roasting on an Open Fire) • Feliz Navidad • I Wonder As I Wander • Mistletoe and Holly • The Most Wonderful Time of the Year • Rockin' Around the Christmas Tree • Santa Claus Is Comin' to Town • Silver Bells • Some Children See Him.

00416790..........$9.99

CHRISTMAS TIME

arr. Carolyn C. Setliff
Mid to Later Intermediate

7 classics: Carol of the Bells • Ding Dong! Merrily on High! • The First Noel • In the Bleak Midwinter • O Holy Night • Sing We Now of Christmas • The Snow Lay on the Ground.

00416713..........$7.99

CHRISTMAS PIANO SOLOS

FIFTH GRADE

arr. Eric Baumgartner
Intermediate to Advanced

10 favorites: Brazilian Sleigh Bells • Christmas Time Is Here • The Christmas Waltz • Frosty the Snow Man • It Must Have Been the Mistletoe (Our First Christmas) • Let It Snow! Let It Snow! Let It Snow! • Rudolph the Red-Nosed Reindeer • We Need a Little Christmas • and more.

00416791..........$11.99

SOLOS FOR THE SANCTUARY – CHRISTMAS

arr. Glenda Austin
Intermediate to Advanced

12 solos: A La Nanita Nana • Away in a Manger • The First Noel • Go, Tell It on the Mountain • God Rest Ye Merry, Gentlemen • He Is Born • Infant Holy, Infant Lowly • Sing We Now of Christmas • What Child Is This? • and more.

00298182..........$12.99

JAZZ IT UP! – CHRISTMAS

arr. Eric Baumgartner
Mid-Intermediate

12 solos: Angels We Have Heard on High • Bring a Torch, Jeannette, Isabella • Coventry Carol • Deck the Hall • Good King Wenceslas • Here We Come A-Caroling • Jesu, Joy of Man's Desiring • Jingle Bells • O Christmas Tree • Ukrainian Bell Carol • and more.

00349037 Book/Audio..........$12.99